Just The

Textbook Key Facts

Textbook Outlines, Highlights, and Practice Quizzes

Essential Algebra for Chemistry Students

by David W. Ball, 2 Edition

All "Just the Facts101" Material Written or Prepared by Cram101 Textbook Reviews

Title Page

LEARNING SYSTEM

"Just the Facts101" is a Content Technologies publication and tool designed to give you all the facts from your textbooks. Register for the full practice test for each of your chapters for virtually any of your textbooks.

Facts101 has built custom study tools specific to your textbook. We provide all of the factual testable information and unlike traditional study guides, we will never send you back to your textbook for more information.

YOU WILL NEVER HAVE TO HIGHLIGHT A BOOK AGAIN!

Facts101 StudyGuides

All of the information in this StudyGuide is written specifically for your textbook. We include the key terms, places, people, and concepts... the information you can expect on your next exam!

Facts101

Only Facts101 gives you the outlines, highlights, and PRACTICE TESTS specific to your textbook. Facts101 sister Cram101.com is an online application where you'll discover study tools designed to make the most of your limited study time.

www.Cram101.com

STUDYING MADE EASY

This Cram101 notebook is designed to make studying easier and increase your comprehension of the textbook material. Instead of starting with a blank notebook and trying to write down everything discussed in class lectures, you can use this Cram101 textbook notebook and annotate your notes along with the lecture.

Our goal is to give you the best tools for success.

For a supreme understanding of the course, pair your notebook with our online tools at www.cram101.com

Our Online Access program is a simple way for us to keep our promise and provide you the best studying tools, regardless of where you purchased your Cram101 textbook notebook. As long as you let us know you are intereested in a free online access account we will set it up for you for 180 days.

Online Access:

SIMPLE STEPS TO GET A FREE ACCOUNT:

Email Travis.Reese@cram101.com

Include:

Order number

ISBN of Guide

Retailer where purchased

Essential Algebra for Chemistry Students
David W. Ball, 2

CONTENTS

1. Numbers, Units, and Scientific Notation

	Number
	Integer
	Negative number
	Constant
	Equation
	Kilogram
	Degree
	Exponent

CHAPTER HIGHLIGHTS & NOTES: KEY TERMS, PEOPLE, PLACES, CONCEPTS

Number	A number is a mathematical object used to count, label, and measure. In mathematics, the definition of number has been extended over the years to include such numbers as 0, negative numbers, rational numbers, irrational numbers, and complex numbers.
	Mathematical operations are certain procedures that take one or more numbers as input and produce a number as output.
Integer	An integer is a number that can be written without a fractional component. For example, 21, 4, 0, and -2048 are integers, while 9.75, 5½, and v
Negative number	A negative number is a real number that is less than zero. Such numbers are often used to represent the amount of a loss or absence. For example, a debt that is owed may be thought of as a negative asset, or a decrease in some quantity may be thought of as a negative increase.
Constant	In mathematics, the adjective constant means non-varying. The noun constant may have two different meanings. It may refer to a fixed and well defined number or other mathematical object.
Equation	In mathematics, an equation is a formula of the form A = B, where A and B are expressions containing one or several variables called unknowns, and '=' denotes the equality binary relation.

1. Numbers, Units, and Scientific Notation

Although written in the form of proposition, an equation is not a statement, but a problem consisting in finding the values, called solutions, that, when substituted to the unknowns, yields equal values of expressions A and B. For example, 2 is the unique solution of the equation x + 2 = 4, in which the unknown is x. Historically, equations arose from the mathematical discipline of algebra, but later become ubiquitous.

Kilogram

The kilogramme, is the base unit of mass in the International System of Units (SI) (the Metric system) and is defined as being equal to the mass of the International Prototype of the Kilogram.

The gram, 1/1000th of a kilogram, was originally defined in 1795 as the mass of one cubic centimeter of water at the melting point of water. The original prototype kilogram, manufactured in 1799 and from which the IPK is derived, had a mass equal to the mass of 1.000028 dm^3 of water at its maximum density at approximately 4 °C.

The kilogram is the only SI base unit with an SI prefix ('kilo', symbol 'k') as part of its name.

Degree

A degree usually denoted by ° (the degree symbol), is a measurement of plane angle, representing $1/360$ of a full rotation. It is not an SI unit, as the SI unit for angles is radian, but it is mentioned in the SI brochure as an accepted unit. Because a full rotation equals 2p radians, one degree is equivalent to p/180 radians.

Exponent

Exponentiation is a mathematical operation, written as b^n, involving two numbers, the base b and the exponent n. When n is a natural number (i.e., a positive integer), exponentiation corresponds to repeated multiplication of the base: that is, b^n is the product of multiplying n

$$b^n = \underbrace{b \times \cdots \times b}_{n}$$

bases:

The exponent is usually shown as a superscript to the right of the base. Some common exponents have their own names: the exponent 2 (or 2nd power) is called the square of b (b^2) or b squared; the exponent 3 (or 3rd power) is called the cube of b (b^3) or b cubed.

1. Numbers, Units, and Scientific Notation

CHAPTER QUIZ: KEY TERMS, PEOPLE, PLACES, CONCEPTS

1. A _____ is a real number that is less than zero. Such numbers are often used to represent the amount of a loss or absence. For example, a debt that is owed may be thought of as a negative asset, or a decrease in some quantity may be thought of as a negative increase.

   a. Number bond
   b. Binary number
   c. Carry
   d. Negative number

2. An _____ is a number that can be written without a fractional component. For example, 21, 4, 0, and -2048 are _____s, while 9.75, 5½, and v

   a. Integer
   b. Circular shift
   c. Clock angle problem
   d. Cognitively Guided Instruction

3. A _____ is a mathematical object used to count, label, and measure. In mathematics, the definition of _____ has been extended over the years to include such _____s as 0, negative _____s, rational _____s, irrational _____s, and complex _____s.

   Mathematical operations are certain procedures that take one or more _____s as input and produce a _____ as output.

   a. Number
   b. Canonical form
   c. Closed-form expression
   d. Cluster algebra

4. In mathematics, the adjective _____ means non-varying. The noun _____ may have two different meanings. It may refer to a fixed and well defined number or other mathematical object.

   a. Basic element
   b. Constant
   c. Canonical form
   d. Closed-form expression

5. . The kilogramme, is the base unit of mass in the International System of Units (SI) (the Metric system) and is defined as being equal to the mass of the International Prototype of the _____.

   The gram, 1/1000th of a _____, was originally defined in 1795 as the mass of one cubic centimeter of water at the melting point of water. The original prototype _____, manufactured in 1799 and from which the IPK is derived, had a mass equal to the mass of 1.000028 dm^3 of water at its maximum density at approximately 4 °C.

1. Numbers, Units, and Scientific Notation

The _____ is the only SI base unit with an SI prefix ('kilo', symbol 'k') as part of its name.

a. Kilogram

b. Microgram

c. Rotation of axes reduced

d. Cubic function

1. d
2. a
3. a
4. b
5. a

You can take the complete Online Interactive Chapter Practice Test

for 1. Numbers, Units, and Scientific Notation
on all key terms, persons, places, and concepts.

No Additional Costs

http://www.Cram101.com

Register, send an email request to Travis.Reese@Cram101.com to get your user Id and password.

Include your customer order number, and ISBN number from your studyguide Retailer.

2. Arithmetic Evaluation

CHAPTER OUTLINE: KEY TERMS, PEOPLE, PLACES, CONCEPTS

	Division
	Logarithm
	Multiplication
	Number
	Subtraction
	Fraction
	Equation
	Equals sign
	Operation
	Operator
	Order of operations
	Expression
	Natural Logarithm

2. Arithmetic Evaluation

Division	In mathematics, especially in elementary arithmetic, division is an arithmetic operation. Specifically, if b times c equals a, written:a = b Ã— c
	where b is not zero, then a divided by b equals c, written:a Ã· b = c
	For instance,6 Ã· 3 = 2
	since3 x 2 = 6
	In the expression a Ã· b = c, a is called the dividend or numerator, b the divisor or denominator and the result c is called the quotient.
	Conceptually, division describes two distinct but related settings.
Logarithm	In mathematics, the logarithm of a number is the exponent to which another fixed value, the base, must be raised to produce that number. For example, the logarithm of 1000 to base 10 is 3, because 10 to the power 3 is 1000: $1000 = 10?×?10?×?10 = 10^3$. More generally, for any two real numbers b and x where b is positive and b ? 1, $y = b^x \Leftrightarrow x = \log_b(y)$
	The logarithm to base 10 (b = 10) is called the common logarithm and has many applications in science and engineering. The natural logarithm has the irrational (transcendental) number e (˜ 2.718) as its base; its use is widespread in pure mathematics, especially calculus.
Multiplication	Multiplication is the mathematical operation of scaling one number by another. It is one of the four basic operations in elementary arithmetic (the others being addition, subtraction and division).
	Because the result of scaling by whole numbers can be thought of as consisting of some number of copies of the original, whole-number products greater than 1 can be computed by repeated addition; for example, 3 multiplied by 4 (often said as '3 times 4') can be calculated by adding 4 copies of 3 together:
	$$3 \times 4 = 3 + 3 + 3 + 3 = 12.$$
	Here 3 and 4 are the 'factors' and 12 is the 'product'.
Number	A number is a mathematical object used to count, label, and measure. In mathematics, the definition of number has been extended over the years to include such numbers as 0, negative numbers, rational numbers, irrational numbers, and complex numbers.

2. Arithmetic Evaluation

Subtraction	Subtraction is a mathematical operation that represents the operation of removing objects from a collection. It is signified by the minus sign (-). For example, in the picture on the right, there are 5 - 2 apples--meaning 5 apples with 2 taken away, which is a total of 3 apples.
Fraction	A fraction represents a part of a whole or, more generally, any number of equal parts. When spoken in everyday English, a fraction describes how many parts of a certain size there are, for example, one-half, eight-fifths, three-quarters. A common, vulgar, or simple fraction consists of an integer numerator, displayed above a line (or before a slash), and a non-zero integer denominator, displayed below (or after) that line.
Equation	In mathematics, an equation is a formula of the form A = B, where A and B are expressions containing one or several variables called unknowns, and '=' denotes the equality binary relation. Although written in the form of proposition, an equation is not a statement, but a problem consisting in finding the values, called solutions, that, when substituted to the unknowns, yields equal values of expressions A and B. For example, 2 is the unique solution of the equation x + 2 = 4, in which the unknown is x. Historically, equations arose from the mathematical discipline of algebra, but later become ubiquitous.
Equals sign	The equals sign or equality sign is a mathematical symbol used to indicate equality. It was invented in 1557 by Robert Recorde. In an equation, the equals sign is placed between two expressions that have the same value.
Operation	The general operation as explained on this page should not be confused with the more specific operators on vector spaces. For a notion in elementary mathematics, see arithmetic operation. In its simplest meaning in mathematics and logic, an operation is an action or procedure which produces a new value from one or more input values, called 'operands'.
Operator	An operator is a mapping from one vector space or module to another. Operators are of critical importance to both linear algebra and functional analysis, and they find application in many other fields of pure and applied mathematics. For example, in classical mechanics, the derivative is used ubiquitously, and in quantum mechanics, observables are represented by hermitian operators.
Order of operations	In mathematics and computer programming, the order of operations is a rule used to clarify which procedures should be performed first in a given mathematical expression. For example, in mathematics and most computer languages multiplication is done before addition; in the expression 2 + 3 -- 4, the answer is 14. Brackets, '(and), { and }, or (and]', which have their own rules, may be used to avoid confusion, thus the preceding expression may also be rendered 2 + (3 -- 4), but the brackets are unnecessary as multiplication still has precedence without them.

2. Arithmetic Evaluation

Expression	In mathematics, an expression is a finite combination of symbols that is well-formed according to rules that depend on the context. Mathematical symbols can designate numbers (constants), variables, operations, functions, punctuation, grouping, and other aspects of logical syntax.
Natural Logarithm	The natural logarithm of a number is its logarithm to the base of the mathematical constant e, where e is an irrational and transcendental number approximately equal to 7000271828182845899?2.718281828459. The natural logarithm of x is generally written as ln x, $\log_e$ x, or sometimes, if the base e is implicit, simply log x. Parentheses are sometimes added for clarity, giving ln(x), $\log_e$(x) or log(x).

1.

   The _____ or equality sign is a mathematical symbol used to indicate equality. It was invented in 1557 by Robert Recorde. In an equation, the _____ is placed between two expressions that have the same value.

   a. Equals sign
   b. Completing the square
   c. Cube root
   d. Cubic function

2. A _____ is a mathematical object used to count, label, and measure. In mathematics, the definition of _____ has been extended over the years to include such _____s as 0, negative _____s, rational _____s, irrational _____s, and complex _____s.

   Mathematical operations are certain procedures that take one or more _____s as input and produce a _____ as output.

   a. Number
   b. Canonical form
   c. Closed-form expression
   d. Cluster algebra

3. . The _____ of a number is its logarithm to the base of the mathematical constant e, where e is an irrational and transcendental number approximately equal to 7000271828182845899?2.718281828459. The _____ of x is generally written as ln x, $\log_e$ x, or sometimes, if the base e is implicit, simply log x. Parentheses are sometimes added for clarity, giving ln(x), $\log_e$(x) or log(x).

a. Rotation of axes reduced
b. algorithm
c. Natural Logarithm
d. identity

4. _____ is the mathematical operation of scaling one number by another. It is one of the four basic operations in elementary arithmetic (the others being addition, subtraction and division).

Because the result of scaling by whole numbers can be thought of as consisting of some number of copies of the original, whole-number products greater than 1 can be computed by repeated addition; for example, 3 multiplied by 4 (often said as '3 times 4') can be calculated by adding 4 copies of 3 together:

$$3 \times 4 = 3 + 3 + 3 + 3 = 12.$$

Here 3 and 4 are the 'factors' and 12 is the 'product'.

a. Negative number
b. Binary number
c. Carry
d. Multiplication

5. In mathematics, especially in elementary arithmetic, _____ is an arithmetic operation. Specifically, if b times c equals a, written: $a = b \times c$

where b is not zero, then a divided by b equals c, written: $a \div b = c$

For instance, $6 \div 3 = 2$

since $3 \times 2 = 6$

In the expression $a \div b = c$, a is called the dividend or numerator, b the divisor or denominator and the result c is called the quotient.

Conceptually, _____ describes two distinct but related settings.

a. Division by two
b. Binary number
c. Carry
d. Division

1. a

2. a

3. c

4. d

5. d

You can take the complete Online Interactive Chapter Practice Test

for 2. Arithmetic Evaluation
on all key terms, persons, places, and concepts.

No Additional Costs

http://www.Cram101.com

Register, send an email request to Travis.Reese@Cram101.com to get your user Id and password.

Include your customer order number, and ISBN number from your studyguide Retailer.

3. Significant Figures

	Significant figures
	Subtraction
	Rounding
	Division
	Multiplication

Significant figures	The significant figures of a number are those digits that carry meaning contributing to its precision. This includes all digits except:•All leading zeros;•Trailing zeros when they are merely placeholders to indicate the scale of the number (exact rules are explained at identifying significant figures); and•Spurious digits introduced, for example, by calculations carried out to greater precision than that of the original data, or measurements reported to a greater precision than the equipment supports. Significance arithmetic are approximate rules for roughly maintaining significance throughout a computation. The more sophisticated scientific rules are known as propagation of uncertainty.
Subtraction	Subtraction is a mathematical operation that represents the operation of removing objects from a collection. It is signified by the minus sign (-). For example, in the picture on the right, there are 5 - 2 apples--meaning 5 apples with 2 taken away, which is a total of 3 apples.
Rounding	Rounding a numerical value means replacing it by another value that is approximately equal but has a shorter, simpler, or more explicit representation; for example, replacing £23.4476 with £23.45, or the fraction 312/937 with 1/3, or the expression v2 with 1.414. Rounding is often done on purpose to obtain a value that is easier to write and handle than the original. It may be done also to indicate the accuracy of a computed number; for example, a quantity that was computed as 123,456 but is known to be accurate only to within a few hundred units is better stated as 'about 123,500.' On the other hand, rounding introduces some round-off error in the result.

3. Significant Figures

Division	In mathematics, especially in elementary arithmetic, division is an arithmetic operation. Specifically, if b times c equals a, written: a = b Ã— c
	where b is not zero, then a divided by b equals c, written: a Ã· b = c
	For instance, 6 Ã· 3 = 2
	since 3 x 2 = 6
	In the expression a Ã· b = c, a is called the dividend or numerator, b the divisor or denominator and the result c is called the quotient.
	Conceptually, division describes two distinct but related settings.
Multiplication	Multiplication is the mathematical operation of scaling one number by another. It is one of the four basic operations in elementary arithmetic (the others being addition, subtraction and division).
	Because the result of scaling by whole numbers can be thought of as consisting of some number of copies of the original, whole-number products greater than 1 can be computed by repeated addition; for example, 3 multiplied by 4 (often said as '3 times 4') can be calculated by adding 4 copies of 3 together: $$3 \times 4 = 3 + 3 + 3 + 3 = 12.$$ Here 3 and 4 are the 'factors' and 12 is the 'product'.

3. Significant Figures

1. The _____ of a number are those digits that carry meaning contributing to its precision. This includes all digits except:•All leading zeros;•Trailing zeros when they are merely placeholders to indicate the scale of the number (exact rules are explained at identifying _____); and•Spurious digits introduced, for example, by calculations carried out to greater precision than that of the original data, or measurements reported to a greater precision than the equipment supports.

    Significance arithmetic are approximate rules for roughly maintaining significance throughout a computation. The more sophisticated scientific rules are known as propagation of uncertainty.

    a. Bracket
    b. Collatz conjecture
    c. Significant figures
    d. Hyperoperation

2. _____ is the mathematical operation of scaling one number by another. It is one of the four basic operations in elementary arithmetic (the others being addition, subtraction and division).

    Because the result of scaling by whole numbers can be thought of as consisting of some number of copies of the original, whole-number products greater than 1 can be computed by repeated addition; for example, 3 multiplied by 4 (often said as '3 times 4') can be calculated by adding 4 copies of 3 together:

    $$3 \times 4 = 3 + 3 + 3 + 3 = 12.$$

    Here 3 and 4 are the 'factors' and 12 is the 'product'.

    a. Multiplication
    b. Binary number
    c. Carry
    d. Chunking

3. . In mathematics, especially in elementary arithmetic, _____ is an arithmetic operation. Specifically, if b times c equals a, written:a = b Ã— c

    where b is not zero, then a divided by b equals c, written:a Ã· b = c

    For instance,6 Ã· 3 = 2

    since3 x 2 = 6

    In the expression a Ã· b = c, a is called the dividend or numerator, b the divisor or denominator and the result c is called the quotient.

    Conceptually, _____ describes two distinct but related settings.

    a. Division by two
    b. Binary number
    c. Carry
    d. Division

4. _____ is a mathematical operation that represents the operation of removing objects from a collection. It is signified by the minus sign (-). For example, in the picture on the right, there are 5 - 2 apples--meaning 5 apples with 2 taken away, which is a total of 3 apples.

    a. Trailing zero
    b. Binary number
    c. Subtraction
    d. Chunking

5. _____ a numerical value means replacing it by another value that is approximately equal but has a shorter, simpler, or more explicit representation; for example, replacing £23.4476 with £23.45, or the fraction 312/937 with 1/3, or the expression v2 with 1.414.

    _____ is often done on purpose to obtain a value that is easier to write and handle than the original. It may be done also to indicate the accuracy of a computed number; for example, a quantity that was computed as 123,456 but is known to be accurate only to within a few hundred units is better stated as 'about 123,500.'

    On the other hand, _____ introduces some round-off error in the result.

    a. Bracket
    b. Rounding
    c. Composite number
    d. Hyperoperation

1. c
2. a
3. d
4. c
5. b

You can take the complete Online Interactive Chapter Practice Test

for 3. Significant Figures
on all key terms, persons, places, and concepts.

No Additional Costs

http://www.Cram101.com

Register, send an email request to Travis.Reese@Cram101.com to get your user Id and password.

Include your customer order number, and ISBN number from your studyguide Retailer.

4. Converting Units

_____	Fraction
_____	Number
_____	Equation
_____	Significant figures

CHAPTER HIGHLIGHTS & NOTES: KEY TERMS, PEOPLE, PLACES, CONCEPTS

Fraction	A fraction represents a part of a whole or, more generally, any number of equal parts. When spoken in everyday English, a fraction describes how many parts of a certain size there are, for example, one-half, eight-fifths, three-quarters. A common, vulgar, or simple fraction consists of an integer numerator, displayed above a line (or before a slash), and a non-zero integer denominator, displayed below (or after) that line.
Number	A number is a mathematical object used to count, label, and measure. In mathematics, the definition of number has been extended over the years to include such numbers as 0, negative numbers, rational numbers, irrational numbers, and complex numbers. Mathematical operations are certain procedures that take one or more numbers as input and produce a number as output.
Equation	In mathematics, an equation is a formula of the form A = B, where A and B are expressions containing one or several variables called unknowns, and '=' denotes the equality binary relation. Although written in the form of proposition, an equation is not a statement, but a problem consisting in finding the values, called solutions, that, when substituted to the unknowns, yields equal values of expressions A and B. For example, 2 is the unique solution of the equation $x + 2 = 4$, in which the unknown is x. Historically, equations arose from the mathematical discipline of algebra, but later become ubiquitous.
Significant figures	The significant figures of a number are those digits that carry meaning contributing to its precision. This includes all digits except:•All leading zeros;•Trailing zeros when they are merely placeholders to indicate the scale of the number (exact rules are explained at identifying significant figures); and•Spurious digits introduced, for example, by calculations carried out to greater precision than that of the original data, or measurements reported to a greater precision than the equipment supports.

4. Converting Units

Significance arithmetic are approximate rules for roughly maintaining significance throughout a computation. The more sophisticated scientific rules are known as propagation of uncertainty.

1. A _____ is a mathematical object used to count, label, and measure. In mathematics, the definition of _____ has been extended over the years to include such _____s as 0, negative _____s, rational _____s, irrational _____s, and complex _____s.

   Mathematical operations are certain procedures that take one or more _____s as input and produce a _____ as output.

   a. Binomial
   b. Number
   c. Closed-form expression
   d. Cluster algebra

2. A _____ represents a part of a whole or, more generally, any number of equal parts. When spoken in everyday English, a _____ describes how many parts of a certain size there are, for example, one-half, eight-fifths, three-quarters. A common, vulgar, or simple _____ consists of an integer numerator, displayed above a line (or before a slash), and a non-zero integer denominator, displayed below (or after) that line.

   a. Canonical form
   b. Fraction
   c. Coefficient
   d. Cluster algebra

3. . The _____ of a number are those digits that carry meaning contributing to its precision. This includes all digits except:•All leading zeros;•Trailing zeros when they are merely placeholders to indicate the scale of the number (exact rules are explained at identifying _____); and•Spurious digits introduced, for example, by calculations carried out to greater precision than that of the original data, or measurements reported to a greater precision than the equipment supports.

   Significance arithmetic are approximate rules for roughly maintaining significance throughout a computation. The more sophisticated scientific rules are known as propagation of uncertainty.

   a. Bracket
   b. Significant figures

4. Converting Units

    c. Composite number

    d. Hyperoperation

4. In mathematics, an _____ is a formula of the form A = B, where A and B are expressions containing one or several variables called unknowns, and '=' denotes the equality binary relation. Although written in the form of proposition, an _____ is not a statement, but a problem consisting in finding the values, called solutions, that, when substituted to the unknowns, yields equal values of expressions A and B. For example, 2 is the unique solution of the _____ x + 2 = 4, in which the unknown is x. Historically, _____s arose from the mathematical discipline of algebra, but later become ubiquitous.

    a. Carlyle circle

    b. Completing the square

    c. Cube root

    d. Equation

1. b
2. b
3. b
4. d

You can take the complete Online Interactive Chapter Practice Test

for 4. Converting Units
on all key terms, persons, places, and concepts.

No Additional Costs

http://www.Cram101.com

Register, send an email request to Travis.Reese@Cram101.com to get your user Id and password.

Include your customer order number, and ISBN number from your studyguide Retailer.

5. Using Chemical Reactions to Make Conversion Factors

	Product
	Number

Product	In mathematics, a product is the result of multiplying, or an expression that identifies factors to be multiplied. The order in which real or complex numbers are multiplied has no bearing on the product; this is known as the commutative law of multiplication. When matrices or members of various other associative algebras are multiplied, the product usually depends on the order of the factors.
Number	A number is a mathematical object used to count, label, and measure. In mathematics, the definition of number has been extended over the years to include such numbers as 0, negative numbers, rational numbers, irrational numbers, and complex numbers. Mathematical operations are certain procedures that take one or more numbers as input and produce a number as output.

1. In mathematics, a _____ is the result of multiplying, or an expression that identifies factors to be multiplied. The order in which real or complex numbers are multiplied has no bearing on the _____; this is known as the commutative law of multiplication. When matrices or members of various other associative algebras are multiplied, the _____ usually depends on the order of the factors.

   a. factor
   b. Product
   c. addend
   d. literal addend

2. . A _____ is a mathematical object used to count, label, and measure.

5. Using Chemical Reactions to Make Conversion Factors

In mathematics, the definition of _____ has been extended over the years to include such _____s as 0, negative _____s, rational _____s, irrational _____s, and complex _____s.

Mathematical operations are certain procedures that take one or more _____s as input and produce a _____ as output.

a. Number
b. Canonical form
c. Closed-form expression
d. Cluster algebra

1. b

2. a

You can take the complete Online Interactive Chapter Practice Test

for 5. Using Chemical Reactions to Make Conversion Factors
on all key terms, persons, places, and concepts.

No Additional Costs

http://www.Cram101.com

Register, send an email request to Travis.Reese@Cram101.com to get your user Id and password.

Include your customer order number, and ISBN number from your studyguide Retailer.

6. Using Mathematical Formulas

	Constant
	Variable
	Quotient
	Spectrum
	Equation

Constant

In mathematics, the adjective constant means non-varying. The noun constant may have two different meanings. It may refer to a fixed and well defined number or other mathematical object.

Variable

In elementary mathematics, a variable is an alphabetic character representing a number, the value of the variable, which is either arbitrary or not fully specified or unknown. Making algebraic computations with variables as if they were explicit numbers allows one to solve a range of problems in a single computation. A typical example is the quadratic formula, which allows to solve every quadratic equation by simply substituting the numeric values of the coefficients of the given equation to the variables that represent them.

Quotient

In mathematics, a quotient is the result of division. For example, when dividing 6 by 3, the quotient is 2, while 6 is called the dividend, and 3 the divisor. The quotient further is expressed as the number of times the divisor divides into the dividend, e.g. 3 divides 2 times into 6. A quotient can also mean just the integer part of the result of dividing two integers.

Spectrum

In functional analysis, the concept of the spectrum of a bounded operator is a generalisation of the concept of eigenvalues for matrices. Specifically, a complex number ? is said to be in the spectrum of a bounded linear operator T if ?I - T is not invertible, where I is the identity operator. The study of spectra and related properties is known as spectral theory, which has numerous applications, most notably the mathematical formulation of quantum mechanics.

Equation

In mathematics, an equation is a formula of the form A = B, where A and B are expressions containing one or several variables called unknowns, and '=' denotes the equality binary relation.

6. Using Mathematical Formulas

Although written in the form of proposition, an equation is not a statement, but a problem consisting in finding the values, called solutions, that, when substituted to the unknowns, yields equal values of expressions A and B. For example, 2 is the unique solution of the equation $x + 2 = 4$, in which the unknown is x. Historically, equations arose from the mathematical discipline of algebra, but later become ubiquitous.

1. In functional analysis, the concept of the _____ of a bounded operator is a generalisation of the concept of eigenvalues for matrices. Specifically, a complex number ? is said to be in the _____ of a bounded linear operator T if ?I - T is not invertible, where I is the identity operator. The study of spectra and related properties is known as spectral theory, which has numerous applications, most notably the mathematical formulation of quantum mechanics.

   a. Spectrum
   b. Dirichlet eigenvalue
   c. Heat kernel
   d. Lax pair

2. In mathematics, a _____ is the result of division. For example, when dividing 6 by 3, the _____ is 2, while 6 is called the dividend, and 3 the divisor. The _____ further is expressed as the number of times the divisor divides into the dividend, e.g. 3 divides 2 times into 6. A _____ can also mean just the integer part of the result of dividing two integers.

   a. 0.999...
   b. Binomial
   c. Canonical form
   d. Quotient

3. In elementary mathematics, a _____ is an alphabetic character representing a number, the value of the _____, which is either arbitrary or not fully specified or unknown. Making algebraic computations with _____s as if they were explicit numbers allows one to solve a range of problems in a single computation. A typical example is the quadratic formula, which allows to solve every quadratic equation by simply substituting the numeric values of the coefficients of the given equation to the _____s that represent them.

   a. Variable
   b. 2 test item
   c. Basic element
   d. Binomial

4. . In mathematics, the adjective _____ means non-varying. The noun _____ may have two different meanings.

It may refer to a fixed and well defined number or other mathematical object.

    a. Basic element
    b. Constant
    c. Canonical form
    d. Closed-form expression

5.   In mathematics, an _____ is a formula of the form A = B, where A and B are expressions containing one or several variables called unknowns, and '=' denotes the equality binary relation. Although written in the form of proposition, an _____ is not a statement, but a problem consisting in finding the values, called solutions, that, when substituted to the unknowns, yields equal values of expressions A and B. For example, 2 is the unique solution of the _____ x + 2 = 4, in which the unknown is x. Historically, _____s arose from the mathematical discipline of algebra, but later become ubiquitous.

    a. Equation
    b. Completing the square
    c. Cube root
    d. Cubic function

1. a
2. d
3. a
4. b
5. a

You can take the complete Online Interactive Chapter Practice Test

for 6. Using Mathematical Formulas
on all key terms, persons, places, and concepts.

No Additional Costs

http://www.Cram101.com

Register, send an email request to Travis.Reese@Cram101.com to get your user Id and password.

Include your customer order number, and ISBN number from your studyguide Retailer.

7. Advanced Math Topics

Exponent

Coefficient

Equation

Quadratic

Quadratic equation

Imaginary number

Number

Quadratic formula

Term

Square

Square root

Cube

Cube root

Base

Function

Exponential function

Logarithm

Natural Logarithm

Quotient

Operation

Significant figures

Exponent	Exponentiation is a mathematical operation, written as b^n, involving two numbers, the base b and the exponent n. When n is a natural number (i.e., a positive integer), exponentiation corresponds to repeated multiplication of the base: that is, b^n is the product of multiplying n bases: $$b^n = \underbrace{b \times \cdots \times b}_{n}$$ The exponent is usually shown as a superscript to the right of the base. Some common exponents have their own names: the exponent 2 (or 2nd power) is called the square of b (b^2) or b squared; the exponent 3 (or 3rd power) is called the cube of b (b^3) or b cubed.
Coefficient	In mathematics, a coefficient is a multiplicative factor in some term of a polynomial, a series or any expression; it is usually a number, but in any case does not involve any variables of the expression. For instance in $$7x^2 - 3xy + 1.5 + y$$ the first two terms respectively have the coefficients 7 and -3. The third term 1.5 is a constant. The final term does not have any explicitly written coefficient, but is considered to have coefficient 1, since multiplying by that factor would not change the term.
Equation	In mathematics, an equation is a formula of the form A = B, where A and B are expressions containing one or several variables called unknowns, and '=' denotes the equality binary relation. Although written in the form of proposition, an equation is not a statement, but a problem consisting in finding the values, called solutions, that, when substituted to the unknowns, yields equal values of expressions A and B. For example, 2 is the unique solution of the equation x + 2 = 4, in which the unknown is x. Historically, equations arose from the mathematical discipline of algebra, but later become ubiquitous.
Quadratic	In mathematics, the term quadratic describes something that pertains to squares, to the operation of squaring, to terms of the second degree, or equations or formulas that involve such terms. Quadratus is Latin for square.
Quadratic equation	In elementary algebra, a quadratic equation is any equation having the form $ax^2 + bx + c = 0$ where x represents an unknown, and a, b, and c represent numbers such that a is not equal to 0. If a = 0, then the equation is linear, not quadratic. The numbers a, b, and c are the coefficients of the equation, and may be distinguished by calling them, respectively, the quadratic coefficient, the linear coefficient and the constant or free term.

7. Advanced Math Topics

Imaginary number	An imaginary number is a number that can be written as a real number multiplied by the imaginary unit i, which is defined by its property $i^2 = -1$. The square of an imaginary number bi is $-b^2$. For example, 5i is an imaginary number, and its square is -25.
Number	A number is a mathematical object used to count, label, and measure. In mathematics, the definition of number has been extended over the years to include such numbers as 0, negative numbers, rational numbers, irrational numbers, and complex numbers. Mathematical operations are certain procedures that take one or more numbers as input and produce a number as output.
Quadratic formula	In basic algebra, the quadratic formula is the solution of the quadratic equation. There are other ways to solve the quadratic equation instead of using the quadratic formula, such as factoring, completing the square, or graphing. Using the quadratic formula is often the most convenient way.
Term	A term is a number or the product of numbers.
Square	In geometry, a square is a regular quadrilateral. This means that it has four equal sides and four equal angles (90-degree angles, or right angles). It can also be defined as a rectangle in which two adjacent sides have equal length.
Square root	In mathematics, a square root of a number a is a number y such that $y^2 = a$, in other words, a number y whose square is a. For example, 4 and -4 are square roots of 16 because $4^2 = (-4)^2 = 16$. Every non-negative real number a has a unique non-negative square root, called the principal square root, which is denoted by v
Cube	In geometry, a cube is a three-dimensional solid object bounded by six square faces, facets or sides, with three meeting at each vertex. The cube can also be called a regular hexahedron and is one of the five Platonic solids. It is a special kind of square prism, of rectangular parallelepiped and of trigonal trapezohedron.
Cube root	In mathematics, a cube root of a number, denoted $\sqrt[3]{x}$ or $x^{1/3}$, is a number a such that $a^3 = x$. All real numbers (except zero) have exactly one real cube root and a pair of complex conjugate roots, and all nonzero complex numbers have three distinct complex cube roots. For example, the real cube root of 8 is 2, because $2^3 = 8$. All the cube roots of -27i are

$$\sqrt[3]{-27i} = \begin{cases} 3i \\ \frac{3\sqrt{3}}{2} - \frac{3}{2}i \\ -\frac{3\sqrt{3}}{2} - \frac{3}{2}i. \end{cases}$$

The cube root operation is not associative or distributive with addition or subtraction.

Base	In geometry, a base is a side of a plane figure or face of a solid, particularly one perpendicular to the direction height is measured or on what is considered to the bottom of the object. This usage can be applied to a triangle, parallelogram, trapezoids, cylinder, cone, pyramid, parallelopiped or frustum. By extension, the length or area of a base is also called a base.
Function	In mathematics, a function is a relation between a set of inputs and a set of permissible outputs with the property that each input is related to exactly one output. An example is the function that relates each real number x to its square x^2. The output of a function f corresponding to an input x is denoted by f(x) (read 'f of x').
Exponential function	In mathematics, an exponential function is a function of the form $f(x) = b^x$ in which the input variable x occurs as an exponent. A function of the form $f(x) = b^{x+c}$ is also considered an exponential function, and a function of the form $f(x) = a \cdot b^x$ can be re-written as $f(x) = b^{x+c}$ by the use of logarithms and so is an exponential function.

Exponential functions are uniquely characterized by the fact that the growth rate of such a function is directly proportional to the value of the function. |
| Logarithm | In mathematics, the logarithm of a number is the exponent to which another fixed value, the base, must be raised to produce that number. For example, the logarithm of 1000 to base 10 is 3, because 10 to the power 3 is 1000: $1000 = 10?\times?10?\times?10 = 10^3$. More generally, for any two real numbers b and x where b is positive and b ? 1, $y = b^x \Leftrightarrow x = \log_b(y)$

The logarithm to base 10 (b = 10) is called the common logarithm and has many applications in science and engineering. The natural logarithm has the irrational (transcendental) number e (̃ 2.718) as its base; its use is widespread in pure mathematics, especially calculus. |
| Natural Logarithm | The natural logarithm of a number is its logarithm to the base of the mathematical constant e, where e is an irrational and transcendental number approximately equal to 70002718281828458997?2.718281828459. The natural logarithm of x is generally written as ln x, $\log_e$ x, or sometimes, if the base e is implicit, simply log x. |

7. Advanced Math Topics

Quotient	In mathematics, a quotient is the result of division. For example, when dividing 6 by 3, the quotient is 2, while 6 is called the dividend, and 3 the divisor. The quotient further is expressed as the number of times the divisor divides into the dividend, e.g. 3 divides 2 times into 6. A quotient can also mean just the integer part of the result of dividing two integers.
Operation	The general operation as explained on this page should not be confused with the more specific operators on vector spaces. For a notion in elementary mathematics, see arithmetic operation. In its simplest meaning in mathematics and logic, an operation is an action or procedure which produces a new value from one or more input values, called 'operands'.
Significant figures	The significant figures of a number are those digits that carry meaning contributing to its precision. This includes all digits except:•All leading zeros;•Trailing zeros when they are merely placeholders to indicate the scale of the number (exact rules are explained at identifying significant figures); and•Spurious digits introduced, for example, by calculations carried out to greater precision than that of the original data, or measurements reported to a greater precision than the equipment supports. Significance arithmetic are approximate rules for roughly maintaining significance throughout a computation. The more sophisticated scientific rules are known as propagation of uncertainty.

1. The _____ of a number are those digits that carry meaning contributing to its precision. This includes all digits except:•All leading zeros;•Trailing zeros when they are merely placeholders to indicate the scale of the number (exact rules are explained at identifying _____); and•Spurious digits introduced, for example, by calculations carried out to greater precision than that of the original data, or measurements reported to a greater precision than the equipment supports.

   Significance arithmetic are approximate rules for roughly maintaining significance throughout a computation. The more sophisticated scientific rules are known as propagation of uncertainty.

   a. Bracket
   b. Collatz conjecture
   c. Composite number
   d. Significant figures

2. .

In geometry, a _____ is a three-dimensional solid object bounded by six square faces, facets or sides, with three meeting at each vertex. The _____ can also be called a regular hexahedron and is one of the five Platonic solids. It is a special kind of square prism, of rectangular parallelepiped and of trigonal trapezohedron.

a. Beer can pyramid
b. Centered cube number
c. Cube
d. Centered dodecahedral number

3. In elementary algebra, a _____ is any equation having the form $ax^2 + bx + c = 0$

where x represents an unknown, and a, b, and c represent numbers such that a is not equal to 0. If a = 0, then the equation is linear, not quadratic. The numbers a, b, and c are the coefficients of the equation, and may be distinguished by calling them, respectively, the quadratic coefficient, the linear coefficient and the constant or free term.

a. Carlyle circle
b. Completing the square
c. Constant term
d. Quadratic equation

4. Exponentiation is a mathematical operation, written as b^n, involving two numbers, the base b and the _____ n. When n is a natural number (i.e., a positive integer), exponentiation corresponds to repeated multiplication of the

$$b^n = \underbrace{b \times \cdots \times b}_{n}$$

base: that is, b^n is the product of multiplying n bases:

The _____ is usually shown as a superscript to the right of the base. Some common _____s have their own names: the _____ 2 (or 2nd power) is called the square of b (b^2) or b squared; the _____ 3 (or 3rd power) is called the cube of b (b^3) or b cubed.

a. Exponent
b. iteriate
c. element
d. stagnant

5. . In mathematics, a _____ is a multiplicative factor in some term of a polynomial, a series or any expression; it is usually a number, but in any case does not involve any variables of the expression. For instance in

$$7x^2 - 3xy + 1.5 + y$$

the first two terms respectively have the _____s 7 and -3. The third term 1.5 is a constant.

7. Advanced Math Topics

The final term does not have any explicitly written _____, but is considered to have _____ 1, since multiplying by that factor would not change the term.

a. Coefficient

b. Binomial

c. Canonical form

d. Closed-form expression

1. d

2. c

3. d

4. a

5. a

You can take the complete Online Interactive Chapter Practice Test

for 7. Advanced Math Topics

on all key terms, persons, places, and concepts.

No Additional Costs

http://www.Cram101.com

Register, send an email request to Travis.Reese@Cram101.com to get your user Id and password.

Include your customer order number, and ISBN number from your studyguide Retailer.

8. Making Graphs

CHAPTER OUTLINE: KEY TERMS, PEOPLE, PLACES, CONCEPTS

	Line
	Slope
	Y-intercept
	Number
	Variable
	Constant
	Extrapolation
	Quadratic
	Quadratic formula

CHAPTER HIGHLIGHTS & NOTES: KEY TERMS, PEOPLE, PLACES, CONCEPTS

Line	The notion of line or straight line was introduced by ancient mathematicians to represent straight objects with negligible width and depth. Lines are an idealization of such objects. Until the seventeenth century, lines were defined like this: 'The line is the first species of quantity, which has only one dimension, namely length, without any width nor depth, and is nothing else than the flow or run of the point which [...] will leave from its imaginary moving some vestige in length, exempt of any width.
Slope	In mathematics, the slope or gradient of a line is a number that describes both the direction and the steepness of the line. Slope is often denoted by the letter m. •The direction of a line is either increasing, decreasing, horizontal or vertical.•A line is increasing if it goes up from left to right.
Y-intercept	In analytic geometry, using the common convention that the horizontal axis represents a variable x and the vertical axis represents a variable y, a y-intercept is a point where the graph of a function or relation intersects with the y-axis of the coordinate system. As such, these points satisfy x = 0.

8. Making Graphs

Number	A number is a mathematical object used to count, label, and measure. In mathematics, the definition of number has been extended over the years to include such numbers as 0, negative numbers, rational numbers, irrational numbers, and complex numbers. Mathematical operations are certain procedures that take one or more numbers as input and produce a number as output.
Variable	In elementary mathematics, a variable is an alphabetic character representing a number, the value of the variable, which is either arbitrary or not fully specified or unknown. Making algebraic computations with variables as if they were explicit numbers allows one to solve a range of problems in a single computation. A typical example is the quadratic formula, which allows to solve every quadratic equation by simply substituting the numeric values of the coefficients of the given equation to the variables that represent them.
Constant	In mathematics, the adjective constant means non-varying. The noun constant may have two different meanings. It may refer to a fixed and well defined number or other mathematical object.
Extrapolation	In mathematics, extrapolation is the process of estimating, beyond the original observation range, the value of a variable on the basis of its relationship with another variable. It is similar to interpolation, which produces estimates between known observations, but extrapolation is subject to greater uncertainty and a higher risk of producing meaningless results. Extrapolation may also mean extension of a method, assuming similar methods will be applicable.
Quadratic	In mathematics, the term quadratic describes something that pertains to squares, to the operation of squaring, to terms of the second degree, or equations or formulas that involve such terms. Quadratus is Latin for square.
Quadratic formula	In basic algebra, the quadratic formula is the solution of the quadratic equation. There are other ways to solve the quadratic equation instead of using the quadratic formula, such as factoring, completing the square, or graphing. Using the quadratic formula is often the most convenient way.

8. Making Graphs

1. In analytic geometry, using the common convention that the horizontal axis represents a variable x and the vertical axis represents a variable y, a _____ is a point where the graph of a function or relation intersects with the y-axis of the coordinate system. As such, these points satisfy x = 0.

   If the curve in question is given as y = f(x), the y-coordinate of the _____ is found by calculating f(0).

   a. Cartesian coordinate system
   b. Y-intercept
   c. Clock angle problem
   d. Cognitively Guided Instruction

2. A _____ is a mathematical object used to count, label, and measure. In mathematics, the definition of _____ has been extended over the years to include such _____s as 0, negative _____s, rational _____s, irrational _____s, and complex _____s.

   Mathematical operations are certain procedures that take one or more _____s as input and produce a _____ as output.

   a. Binomial
   b. Canonical form
   c. Closed-form expression
   d. Number

3. In mathematics, the term _____ describes something that pertains to squares, to the operation of squaring, to terms of the second degree, or equations or formulas that involve such terms. Quadratus is Latin for square.

   a. quartic
   b. Rotation of axes reduced
   c. Quadratic
   d. Closed-form expression

4. In mathematics, the adjective _____ means non-varying. The noun _____ may have two different meanings. It may refer to a fixed and well defined number or other mathematical object.

   a. Basic element
   b. Constant
   c. Canonical form
   d. Closed-form expression

5. . In elementary mathematics, a _____ is an alphabetic character representing a number, the value of the _____, which is either arbitrary or not fully specified or unknown. Making algebraic computations with _____s as if they were explicit numbers allows one to solve a range of problems in a single computation.

8. Making Graphs

A typical example is the quadratic formula, which allows to solve every quadratic equation by simply substituting the numeric values of the coefficients of the given equation to the _____s that represent them.

a. 1 test item
b. 2 test item
c. Variable
d. Binomial

ANSWER KEY
8. Making Graphs

1. b
2. d
3. c
4. b
5. c

You can take the complete Online Interactive Chapter Practice Test

for 8. Making Graphs
on all key terms, persons, places, and concepts.

No Additional Costs

http://www.Cram101.com

Register, send an email request to Travis.Reese@Cram101.com to get your user Id and password.

Include your customer order number, and ISBN number from your studyguide Retailer.